93

GW00514634

E203091965 2 001

SIMPLE CASH BOOKS FOR SMALL BUSINESSES

SIMPLE CASH BOOKS FOR SMALL BUSINESSES

Second Edition

Paul D Ordidge

KOGAN
PAGE

ESSEX COUNTY LIBRARY

Copyright © Paul D Ordidge 1986, 1989

All rights reserved

First published in Great Britain in 1986
by Kogan Page Ltd, 120 Pentonville Road,
London N1 9JN
Second edition 1989

British Library Cataloguing in Publication Data

Ordidge, Paul D.
   Simple cash books for small businesses.
   1. Great Britain. Small firms. Bookkeeping
   I. Title
   657′.2

   ISBN 1-85091-975-5

Typeset by DP Photosetting, Aylesbury, Bucks
Printed and bound in Great Britain by
Richard Clay (The Chaucer Press), Bungay

GW54525

Contents

Introduction

The aim of this book is to give a basic grounding in simple bookkeeping and cash control, suitable for self-employed people and small businesses that cannot afford or are not interested in a computer, and new students of accountancy.

As a practising accountant, I find that I am constantly answering the same basic questions regarding the requirements of an adequate bookkeeping system. This book answers all of those queries in a way that avoids unnecessary accounting jargon, so it should be understood by all.

In order to simplify things as much as possible, the book concentrates on the requirements of a small business which operates without taking or giving credit on a large scale. Thus the added complications of day books and ledgers can be ignored.

Chapters are included on the popular pre-printed Cash Books and on the bookkeeping treatment of Value Added Tax.

There is no doubt that computers can be a very useful tool in competent hands, but they are expensive. For a small company which has the resources to cover an expenditure of around £1500 upwards and which has the volume of transactions to justify that sort of outlay, a computer may well be a good buy.

The following points need to be borne in mind, however:

1. It is a mistake to think that pressing a few buttons is going to solve all your bookkeeping problems. You still need a basic grounding in bookkeeping technique in order to understand the information that a computer will throw at you.
2. Computers are only as good as the programs which go into them. Program designers are not necessarily accountants and therefore many programs that you can buy will give disappointing results.
3. Until you are thoroughly familiar with your machine and its program the simplest jobs will take a long time to do and this can be a problem if you cannot afford a full-time bookkeeper or computer operator.
4. The so-called 'home computers' are relatively cheap. However, to be of any use for business, a good quality printer, which is

expensive, will also be needed. Also, the quality and speed of the programs for these machines is restricted by the use of magnetic tape. For practical bookkeeping, it is almost essential to use disk storage which again is expensive. However, it is also true that computing costs are reducing all the time in real terms.

This book has been designed with specific circumstances in mind so that the individual reader can concentrate only on the parts that affect his or her business. In this way it is hoped that he or she will not be put off by complications that do not concern them.

Remember that simple bookkeeping is largely a matter of common sense and following simple logical steps. The preparation of accounts and financial statements is something quite different and is usually best left to the experts. You can reduce their costs by keeping your books in good order.

What is a Cash Book?

A Cash Book is a daily record of all monies received and paid out by the business.

It should show, in the case of receipts:

1. The date of receipt of the money
2. From whom the money was received
3. The amount received
4. What the money was received for

and in the case of payments:

1. The date of the payment
2. The name of the person paid
3. The amount paid
4. What the payment was for.

All the above information should be written down as a list in date order.

An 'Analysed Cash Book' takes the basic list a stage further by showing what each receipt or payment is for and recording the information in such a way that it can be seen at a glance exactly how much money has been received for Sales, Tax Refunds, VAT Refunds etc, or paid out for Purchases of Materials, Wages, Motor Expenses, Rent and Rates, Insurance etc.

The Cash Book must also show how payments have been made as there are numerous methods of making them, such as:

1. Cheque
2. Cash

3. Credit Card
4. Bank Standing Order or Direct Debit
5. Bank Draft

to name the most common forms of payment.

What type of Cash Book should I keep?

This really depends on the size of your business and the volume of transactions that you need to record each week.

If you have few transactions each week then you can do a lot worse than to buy one of the pre-printed Cash Books, such as the Simplex D or the Evrite Cash Book, where the required analysis is clearly laid out on each page and each page is intended to record a week's transactions.

The main points to look out for when using one of these Cash Books are set out in Chapter 7 (on page 49).

If the number of transactions per week is too large for you to use a pre-printed Cash Book easily, then you will need to buy a 'columnar Cash Book', ie a book with empty lined pages divided up into a number of columns.

The following chapters are designed to show you how to prepare your own analysis using one of these books.

It would be advisable to buy a book with at least 18 columns per page for recording payments and a second book with, say, 9 or 10 columns for recording receipts.

Whichever type of book you intend to use, any good stationer will be able to supply you with what you need.

Having obtained our book we now proceed to business.

Chapter 1

Recording Payments by Cheque

This chapter assumes that we have opted for preparing our own Analysed Cash Book and that we have bought a suitable one with at least 18 columns per page.

We shall first deal with recording cheque payments in this chapter and show how to record cash payments in Chapter 2.

You can either use two separate books for cheque payments and cash payments, or record cheque payments in the front of a book working forwards and cash payments in the back of the same book working backwards, or vice versa.

Payments by cheque

Stage 1

Set out your column headings at the top of your Cash Book as shown in Figure 1 on page 12.

Note that the following columns should be shown for all businesses:

Date	Supplier (name)	Invoice number	Cheque number	Total amount	Cash drawn

The remaining headings can be adjusted to suit your particular circumstances. For instance, if you are running a shop and do not need to advertise regularly, there is little point in wasting a column for Advertising expenditure. If the odd advertising expense occurs, you can record the amount in the Sundry Expenses column, ensuring that you make a note that the payment was for advertising.

Example

Total amount £				Sundry expenses £	
50.00				50.00	Advert

Where you make regular payments for certain types of expenditure, however, it is advisable to allocate a column to each category of expense.

It is common practice to include Rent, Rates and Insurance payments in the same column, as such payments tend to be regular but infrequent.

Capital items, for example a new car, electric calculator, shop till etc, can usually be conveniently included in the Sundry Expenses column, as these are normally one-off payments. Remember to make a note of exactly what you have bought if you do record the payment in the Sundry Expenses column. This will make the subsequent analysis by your accountant so much easier. See item 4 on page 45.

In the Cash Drawn column insert the amount of money that you have drawn out of the bank in order to buy things with cash. This amount will also be shown as 'Cash Received' in the separate book dealing with cash transactions.

At the end of each week

Do not put your bookkeeping off. You will be surprised how very quickly it can become an unbearable burden if you do not make the necessary entries at regular intervals. A period of one week is usually enough for most small businesses. Larger businesses may require daily attention.

Stage 2

From your cheque stubs, write down the details as required by each column of your Cash Book, as shown in Figure 1.

The payments should be listed in cheque numerical order to ensure that you do not miss out a payment by mistake.

If you cancel a cheque, always record the cheque number in the normal sequence in the Cash Book, leaving the Total Amount column blank and writing 'Cheque Cancelled' in the Supplier Name column.

Stage 3

If you make Standing Order or Direct Debit payments from your bank account, write down the relevant amount as you would for a cheque payment in the week in which your bank normally charges your account. This is easy to find out by merely looking at the date of the payment for that Standing Order on your last bank statement.

Write the letters S/O in the Cheque Number column to indicate that the payment is by Standing Order.

The difference between a Standing Order and a Direct Debit is that the person who is being paid can ask the bank to alter a Direct Debit payment without the payee's permission, provided that the paying authority continues. With a Standing Order, a change in the amount to be paid requires a new payment mandate.

Figure 1. *Payments through a bank account*

Date (Day/Month)	Supplier	Invoice number	Cheque number	Total amount	Cash drawn	Purchases	Motor travel
				£	£	£	£
2/3	Mrs Smith	1	100110	100.00		100.00	
2/3	Cash		111	100.00	100.00		
3/3	Road Tax Car		112	100.00			100.00
5/3	Hire Purchase Instal		S/O	85.00			
5/3	HB Cash & Carry	2	113	75.00			
6/3	GB Telecom	3	114	36.00			
6/3	Oxbridge Herald	4	115	33.00			
	Total W/E 6/3			529.00	100.00	100.00	100.00
9/3	Bert's Insurance	5	116	112.00			
9/3	"	6	117	80.00			80.00
9/3	Mr James	7	118	95.00		95.00	
11/3	Cash		119	70.00	70.00		
12/3	Fred's Furnishing	8	120	120.00			
12/3	Smith's Stationers	9	302201	6.00			
12/3	Inland Revenue	10	202	250.00			
13/3	Electricity Board	11	203	82.00			
	Total W/E 13/3			815.00	70.00	95.00	80.00
16/3	Cash		204	70.00	70.00		
16/3	Mrs Smith	12	205	150.00		150.00	
19/3	Oxbridge Council	13	206	200.00			
19/3	Water Rates	14	207	50.00			
19/3	Bob's Garage	15	208	75.00			75.00
20/3	Barclaycard	16	209	100.00			30.00
20/3	Oxbridge Herald	17	210	33.00			
	Cheque Cancelled		211				
	Total W/E 20/3			678.00	70.00	150.00	105.00
23/3	Gas Board	18	212	35.00			
24/3	Parking Fine	19	213	6.00			6.00
25/3	Supermarket	20	214	25.00			
25/3	Bank Charges			3.50			
27/3	Bank Interest			17.00			
27/3	Accountant	21	215	95.00			
	Total W/E 27/3			181.50	–	–	6.00
	Page Total			2,203.50	240.00	345.00	291.00

S/O = Standing Order
W/E = Week ending

Rent/Rates insurance £	Light/ heat £	Tele- phone £	S/O charges £	Print/Stat. postage £	Adver- tising £	Own drawings £	Sundry expenses £
			85.00				75.00 Calculator
		36.00					
					33.00		
–	–	36.00	85.00	–	33.00	–	75.00
112.00							
				6.00		(Chair for Home) 120.00	
						(Income Tax) 250.00	
	82.00						
112.00	82.00	–	–	6.00	–	370.00	–
200.00							
50.00							
					(New Suit) 60.00		10.00
					33.00		
250.00	–	–	–	–	33.00	60.00	10.00
	35.00						
			3.50				
			17.00				
						(Own Food) 25.00	
							95.00 Accountant
–	35.00	–	20.50	–	–	25.00	95.00
362.00	117.00	36.00	105.50	6.00	66.00	455.00	180.00

Stage 4

When you have recorded all the payments for the week, add up each column and pencil in each total on the next clear line down in your Cash Book.

To ensure that your addition is correct and also to ensure that you have correctly extended the amounts from the Total Amount column into the relevant analysis column, add up the totals of the analysis columns and check that the result comes to the total of the Total Amount column.

If it does not:

1. Check that for each figure in the Total Amount column you have figures in the analysis columns which add up to that total.
2. If the first check does not highlight your mistake, you have made an addition error in one or more of the columns. Check the addition of the Total Amount column first and then each of the others until you find your mistake.

At the end of your accounting year your accountant will require the totals of all the weekly totals in order to prepare your accounts. You can help him to do this and at the same time keep a close eye on how much your business is costing you, by totalling the weekly totals periodically and recording the running total.

It may be more convenient to total each month's payments (especially if you are registered for Value Added Tax, dealt with in Chapter 8).

In Figure 1, one month's payments happen to fit on to one page of our Cash Book. Therefore, our page totals also represent one month's payments.

Stage 5

When you have completed recording the details of your payments in the Cash Book, you must then reference and file the receipts (invoices) which relate to each payment.

This is extremely important as you may be called upon by the Inland Revenue (and by the Customs and Excise, if you are VAT registered) to present evidence of the expense claims that you make.

Referencing

The simplest way to reference your receipts is shown in Figure 1. Start at the beginning of your accounting year with the first payment for which you have a receipt.

Write a large number 1 in the top right-hand corner of the receipt and write the same number in the Invoice Number column of your Cash

Book next to the payment to which the receipt relates.

The second receipt of the year will be numbered 2 and so on. For some payments you will not have a receipt:

(a) Cash drawn from a bank account
(b) Hire purchase instalments
(c) Bank charges and interest
(d) Road Tax on your car.

Where this is the case, leave the Invoice Number column blank. Only use a number when you have a receipt, so as to maintain a constant numerical sequence.

Filing receipts

There are many ways of doing this. Provided that each receipt can be quickly and easily found, it does not matter how you choose to store your receipts.

For businesses which make few payments each week, one method is: after referencing, to staple each week's receipts together and put them in an envelope. You will have an envelope for each week's receipts and each envelope must be marked with the date of its weekend.

For businesses where the number of receipts makes this method impractical, lever arch files, or some similar 'ring' type file should be used. This method can, of course, be used by any size of business and is probably to be preferred as it is less likely that receipts will be lost.

Bank statement

Stage 6

On receipt of your bank statement, which may be as frequently as you request, you must examine the period covered by the statement to ensure that there are no NON-CHEQUE items on the statement that you have not recorded in your Cash Book. It may be, for instance, that Bank Charges and Interest have been charged to your account. If so, you must record the payment in your Cash Book.

The instructions given above, if followed correctly, will leave you with a complete record of your payments through the bank in the form shown by Figure 1 (on pages 12–13).

There is no need for you to take the next step unless you wish to, which is to reconcile your Cash Book with your bank statement, as this will be done by your accountant at the end of the year.

By bank reconciliation we mean checking that all the items on your bank statements are correctly recorded in your Cash Book.

This technique therefore ensures that you have not made any mistakes in recording transactions in your Cash Book relating to payments and receipts passing through your bank account.

This step can be surprisingly complicated and it is usually not worth losing sleep over, should you be unable to agree your records with your bank records.

I have explained the technique in Chapter 5 for those who feel that they want to try to use it.

Chapter 2
Recording Payments in Cash

Recording payments in cash in a 'columnar Cash Book' is similar to recording cheques as shown in Chapter 1, with a few minor simplifications.

If you have only one Cash Book and have used the front for cheques paid, then start at the back of the book for cash payments and work forward.

Payments in cash

Stage 1
Set out your Cash Book headings as shown in Figure 2 (on pages 18–19). As already mentioned in the chapter on cheque payments, the choice of analysis columns depends on the requirements of the individual business. However, all businesses should have the following standard columns:

Date	Supplier (name)	Invoice number	Total amount £

You can then allocate the remaining columns in your Cash Book according to the type of expenses that you normally pay with cash.

As with the infrequent cheque payments, payments for such things as capital equipment (explained in Chapter 6) can be conveniently recorded in the Sundry Expenses column rather than allocating a column which may only be used for one or two entries. This avoids wasting space.

Stage 2
Cash payments present an additional difficulty because you do not have the convenience of a cheque book stub from which to write up your Cash Book. No one is perfect and it is quite likely that you will miss out payments by accident, especially if you do not have a receipt.

The consequences of missing out one or more payments could be that your accountant will have to increase the figure for your own Drawings at the end of the year by the difference between your total business income and your cash payments plus amounts paid into your bank

Figure 2. *Payments in cash*

Date (Day/Month)	Supplier	Invoice number	Total amount	Purchases	Motor travel
			£	£	£
2/3	Self Drawings		60.00		
2/3	Post Office—NI		4.25		
3/3	Petrol	1	15.00		15.00
3/3	Rent of Premises		10.00		
3/3	Life Assurance		2.00		
4/3	Mr Jackson	2	30.00	30.00	
4/3	”	3	45.00	45.00	
5/3	Post Office—Stamps		5.00		
6/3	Jim's Wages		20.00		
6/3	Pocket Calculator	4	5.00		
	Total W/E 6/3		196.25	75.00	15.00
9/3	Self Drawings		60.00		
9/3	Post Office—NI		4.25		
9/3	Mr Jackson	5	35.00	35.00	
9/3	Rent of Premises		10.00		
9/3	Life Assurance		2.00		
10/3	Paraffin for Heater	6	5.00		
11/3	Petrol	7	17.00		17.00
13/3	Jim's Wages		20.00		
	Total W/E 13/3		153.25	35.00	17.00
16/3	Self Drawings		60.00		
16/3	Post Office—NI		4.25		
17/3	Rent of Premises		10.00		
17/3	Life Assurance		2.00		
18/3	Gift		70.00		
19/3	Church Magazine—Advert		7.50		
20/3	Jim's Wages		20.00		
	Total W/E 20/3		173.75	—	—
23/3	Self Drawings		60.00		
23/3	Post Office—NI		4.25		
25/3	Petrol	8	10.00		10.00
25/3	Car MOT	9	6.00		6.00
25/3	Rent of Premises		10.00		
25/3	Life Assurance		2.00		
27/3	Jim's Wages		20.00		
	Total W/E 27.3		112.25	—	16.00
	Page Total		635.50	110.00	48.00

Rent	Light/heat	Print/Stat. postage	Advertising	Staff wages	Drawings	Sundry expenses
£	£	£	£	£	£	£
					60.00	
					4.25	
10.00						
					2.00	
		5.00				
				20.00		
						5.00
10.00	–	5.00	–	20.00	66.25	5.00
					60.00	
					4.25	
10.00						
	5.00				2.00	
				20.00		
10.00	5.00	–	–	20.00	66.25	–
					60.00	
					4.25	
10.00						
					2.00	
					70.00	
			7.50			
				20.00		
10.00	–	–	7.50	20.00	136.25	–
					60.00	
					4.25	
10.00						
					2.00	
				20.00		
10.00	–	–	–	20.00	66.25	–
40.00	5.00	5.00	7.50	80.00	335.00	5.00

account. As a result, your profit for the year could be overstated and you could be paying more tax than is necessary.

It is therefore in your best interests to ensure that you account for every business cash payment.

Ideally, you should obtain a receipt for each payment. If for any reason this is not possible, make out your own receipt by jotting down the date of payment, the name of the person paid, or the product bought and the amount paid. You can do this on any scrap of paper, or you can buy Petty Cash slips from any stationers.

Keep all your cash receipts and rough notes in a box separately from the receipts that you obtain for your cheque payments. It is advisable to mark all cash receipts with a large letter 'C' as you pay them if there is any danger of mixing cash receipts with cheque receipts.

Weekly, or at the end of each period in which you normally write up your Cash Book, empty your box of cash receipts and write down the necessary details from the receipts into your Cash Book, as shown in Figure 2.

Referencing and filing receipts

Stage 3
Reference each of the receipts in the same way as shown for cheque receipts (on page 15).

By filing your cash receipts separately from your cheque receipts, you can use the same reference number system, that is starting at number 1 then number 2, and so on.

Keep all receipts in weekly envelopes marked with the date of the weekend, or in lever arch or ring files.

Checking

Stage 4
At the end of each week, add up all the columns and pencil in each total on the next line down in your Cash Book.

To ensure that your addition is correct and that you have not made any mistakes in your analysis columns, add up all the totals of the analysis columns to ensure that they equal the total of the Total Amount column.

If they do not:

1. Check that each figure in the Total Amount column has a corresponding figure in one of the analysis columns.

2. If the first check does not reveal your mistake you have made an addition error in one or more of the columns. Check the addition of the Total Amount column first and then each column in turn until you find the mistake.

It is also advisable to note each month's totals, particularly if you are registered for VAT. You could also keep a running total of each column throughout the year, which will assist your accountant.

Note that the total of the analysis columns must always be equal to the total of the Total Amount column, whether you are doing your additions weekly, monthly, or keeping a running total throughout the year.

Chapter 3
Recording Income (or Receipts)

There are many ways of recording your business income, depending on the type of business that you are running and the way in which you deal with cash.

The following notes and suggested column headings for your Cash Book are intended as a guide, given various possible situations. You should adopt the method which best suits your particular circumstances. Methods 1 and 2 can be used whether you give your customer an invoice or not.

Five recording methods explained

Method 1
Suitable if you receive relatively large amounts from a few, known customers and you pay all amounts received into your bank account:

Date	Customer (name)	Invoice number	Sales/ Takings (amount) £	Sundry receipts* £	Amount banked £

*See note 2 on page 23.

Method 2
As for Method 1, except that you use cash received to pay some of your expenses and bank the remainder:

Date	Customer	Invoice number	Sales/ Takings £	Sundry receipts £	Cash used for expenses £	Amount banked £

Method 3
Suitable if you receive a large number of relatively small amounts from customers who you do not know by name, for example as in a shop; you use a till and you bank all your takings:

Date	Amount in till at start £	Amount in till at end £	Sundry receipts £	Amount banked £	Takings amount £

Method 4

As for Method 3, except that you use money from the till to pay for expenses and bank the remainder:

Date	Amount in till at start £	Amount in till at end £	Cash used for expenses £	Sundry receipts £	Amount banked £	Takings amount £

Method 5

Suitable for subcontractors in the building industry who do not hold an Exemption Certificate and consequently suffer tax at the basic rate which is deducted from their gross pay by the main contractor:

Date	Contractor (name)	Amounts shown by stubs			Sundry receipts £	Amount banked £
		Gross £	SC60 tax £	Net £		

In all the above methods it is assumed that you do not give your customers a period of credit in which to pay and therefore you write your invoice details into your Cash Book only as the money is received.

If your invoices are not pre-numbered, you should reference your copy of the invoice with a number sequence of your own. Each invoice number should be shown in the Invoice Number column of your Cash Book next to the relevant receipt.

The main points to note are:

1. In Methods 1, 2 and 5, you record the names of your customers and show the separate amounts received from each.
2. In each method there is a column for Sundry Receipts, that is receipts which do not arise from a sale of your business goods or services. For instance, you may receive a tax rebate, or insurance refund. These amounts should be shown in the Sundry Receipts column.
3. For Methods 1 and 2, you would normally give your customer a sales invoice (receipt) and keep a carbon copy for yourself as evidence of the sale.

    For Methods 3 and 4, there will usually be a till roll which should be kept as evidence of your sales.

    For Method 5, you must keep the SC60 slips as evidence that basic rate tax has been deducted from your receipts.

For the purposes of our worked example in Figure 3 (on pages 24–25), we have assumed that we run our business from shop premises and do not relate specific receipts to particular customers; that we have a till for

Figure 3. *Receipts*

Date	1 Amount in till at start £	2 Amount in till at end £	3 Cash used for expenses £	4 Sundry receipts £	5 Amount banked £	6 Takings amount £
2/3	50.00	15.00	64.25	—	—	29.25
3/3	15.00	70.00	—	—	—	55.00
4/3	70.00	98.00	2.00	—	—	30.00
5/3	98.00	138.00	5.00	—	—	45.00
6/3	138.00	63.00	25.00	—	100.00	50.00
	50.00	63.00	96.25	—	100.00	209.25
9/3	63.00	42.60	111.25	50.00	—	40.85
10/3	42.60	67.60	5.00	—	—	30.00
11/3	67.60	92.60	—	—	—	25.00
12/3	92.60	92.60	—	—	100.00	—
13/3	92.60	22.60	—	—	—	30.00
	63.00	22.60	116.25	50.00	100.00	125.85

Date						
16/3	22.60	77.60	—	—	—	55.00
17/3	77.60	147.60	—	—	—	70.00
18/3	147.60	192.20	56.25	—	—	100.85
19/3	192.20	234.70	7.50	—	—	50.00
20/3	234.70	39.70	20.00	—	250.00	75.00
	22.60	39.70	83.75	—	250.00	350.85
23/3	39.70	41.30	64.25	—	—	65.85
24/3	41.30	91.30	—	—	—	50.00
25/3	91.30	123.30	28.00	20.00	—	40.00
26/3	123.30	158.30	—	—	—	35.00
27/3	158.30	33.30	20.00	—	150.00	45.00
	39.70	33.30	112.25	20.00	150.00	235.85
Page Total	50.00	33.30	408.50	70.00	600.00	921.80

holding cash; and that we draw cash from the till to pay for some of our expenses and bank the remainder.

Thus Method 4 is appropriate, which is the most complicated method to follow.

Methods 1, 2 and 5 merely require the details to be written down straight into your Cash Book.

Note that the amount banked should be the sum of your Takings and Sundry Receipts, from the date that you last paid money into the bank:

Example

Date	Customer	Invoice number	Takings amount £	Sundry receipts £	Amount banked £
1/3	W	4	100.00		100.00
2/3	X	5	150.00		
3/3	Y	6	150.00		
4/3	Z	7	100.00		
5/3	Insurance refund			50.00	450.00

If Method 2 were being used and we used £50.00 out of the £150.00 received from customer X on 2/3 (2 March), for paying expenses, the amount banked figure on 5/3 (5 March) would be £400.00.

Example

Date	Customer	Invoice number	Takings amount £	Sundry receipts £	Cash used for expenses £	Amount banked £
1/3	W	4	100.00			100.00
2/3	X	5	150.00		(50.00)	
3/3	Y	6	150.00			
4/3	Z	7	100.00			
5/3	Insurance refund			50.00		400.00

NB. Cash Used for Expenses has been deducated from Takings plus Sundry Receipts to arrive at the Amount Banked on 5/3.

Procedure for recording income by method 4 each day:

Stage 1

Count the cash in the till at the beginning of the day, before opening for business. Record this amount in the appropriate column of the Cash Book as shown in Figure 3.

Stage 2

If you draw any cash out of the till for paying expenses during the day, write down the amount that you draw on a piece of paper and put it in the till. This is a reminder of the amount that you drew out. Human memory being what it is, if you do not do this, by the end of the day you will probably have forgotten how much you drew.

Stage 3

At the end of each day, count the amount of money in the till. Record that amount in the appropriate column of the Cash Book.

It has been assumed that during Friday 6/3 (6 March) in Figure 3, you went to the bank and paid in £100.00, so that the amount left in the till on Friday evening is much lower than the amount that you started the day with.

Clearly, the closing cash in till on Monday evening should be the same as the opening cash in till on Tuesday morning. Thus Tuesday's closing cash in till is Wednesday's opening cash in till and so on.

Stage 4

After slotting into the appropriate columns the figures obtained above, you arrive at the Takings for the day as follows:

ADD: Cash in Till   +   Cash Used for   +   Amount Banked
          at End   Expenses

and from this result

DEDUCT: Cash in Till at Start

The result is the day's Takings which should then be recorded in the Takings column.

If your till has an efficient till roll the total sales shown by the till roll should equal the figure arrived at by the above calculation.

Stage 5

If you have a Sundry Receipt, that is a receipt which does not arise from your normal business activities, such as an insurance refund, you must enter the amount received in the Sundry Receipts column as shown in Figure 3 for the £50.00 received on 9/3 (9 March).

One further stage to the above calculation then has to be performed in order to arrive at the Takings/Sales figure for the day:

DEDUCT: Sundry Receipts from the result obtained above
          (in Stage 4).

Thus in Figure 3 the Takings figure of £40.00 on 9/3 was arrived at as follows:

Cash in till at end £		Cash used for expenses £		Amount banked £		Cash in till at start £		Sundry receipts £		Takings amount £
42.60	+	111.25	+	NIL	–	63.00	–	50.00	=	40.85

Stage 6

At the end of each week you should add up columns 3, 4, 5 and 6 and pencil in the totals on the next line down in the Cash Book.

In the place where the total for column 1 would be, you pencil in the Cash in Till at the start of the week, that is, in Figure 3, for the week ending 6/3, we enter £50.00.

In the place where the total for column 2 would be you pencil in the Cash in Till at the end of the week, that is £63.00 for the week ending 6/3.

You then add or subtract the totals of the columns by number as indicated in Figure 3, as follows:

$$\text{Columns } 2 + 3 + 5 - 4 - 1 = \text{Column } 6$$

So, for the week ending 6/3:

$$63.00 + 96.25 + 100.00 - \text{NIL} - 50.00 = 209.25$$

If you do the above calculation and the result of column 6 does not come to the same figure obtained by adding up column 6 (£209.25 in the example) then you should first check the additions of columns 3 to 6, and if this does not reveal the answer, check each day's calculation according to the formula given above.

It is useful to record the totals of columns 3, 4, 5 and 6 for each month as well as each week, particularly if you are VAT registered. You can also keep a running total of each of those columns throughout the year if you wish. This enables you to see how well you are doing as the year progresses and reduces the work that will need to be done by your accountant at the end of the year.

Chapter 4

How to Control Your Cash Expenditure

This is not an easy thing to do. There are few people who can say with complete conviction that they can account for every penny that they spend. Nevertheless, it is important to make an effort as the result of failing to record a business payment is that profits are overstated and your tax bill will be higher than it should be.

The way to control your cash expenditure is first and foremost, to obtain a receipt for everything that you buy with cash. If you cannot obtain a receipt, make your own as a reminder that you have spent the money.

You can check on the accuracy of your cash records by constructing a Cash Control Account. This can be done daily, weekly, monthly or annually, but it is advisable to leave a gap of no more than a week, as you will almost certainly forget what you spent during the week if you do.

Figure 4 (on pages 30-31) shows the construction of a Cash Control Account for each of the four weeks in March from the example used in the previous chapters.

The Cash in Till at the start and end of the week is arrived at simply by counting the cash in the till. The remaining figures are obtained from the appropriate figures in your Cash Book, as indicated in Figures 2 and 3.

Main points to note

1. *You may keep cash in more than one place.* The opening and closing cash balance each week should be the total of all cash held, whether it be in the till, in your pocket or in a Petty Cash box.

The only exception to this is the money that you have paid yourself as wages, that is your Drawings. This money is no longer business money. It is for your private expenses and should be kept separately.

Thus in Figure 3 (pages 24-25) at the end of the second week 13/3, we had £22.60 in the till and £33.00 remaining of the £116.25 taken from the till during the week to pay for business expenses.

Many people with small businesses, particularly where a till is not used, tend to keep cash in their pockets and pay for both private and business expenses out of the same fund.

Figure 4. *Cash control accounts*

	£	£
Cash in Till at start of week		50.00
Add Receipts: Takings		209.25
Sundry		—
Cash drawn from bank		100.00
		359.25
Deduct Payments: Cash paid into bank	100.00	
Cash Expenses per Cash Book	196.25	(296.25)
Cash in Till at end of week 6/3		63.00
Add Receipts: Takings		125.85
Sundry		50.00
Cash drawn from bank		70.00
		308.85
Deduct Payments: Cash paid into bank	100.00	
Cash Expenses per Cash Book	153.25	(253.25)
Cash in Till at end of week 13/3		22.60

Cash in Pocket at end of week 13/3   33.00

Add Receipts: Takings   350.85
                  Sundry   —
                  Cash drawn from bank   70.00

                                                                     476.45

Deduct payments: Cash paid into bank   250.00
                  Cash Expenses per Cash Book   173.75   (423.75)

Cash in Till at end of week 20/3   39.70
Cash in Pocket at end of week 20/3   13.00

Add Receipts: Takings   235.85
                  Sundry   20.00
                  Cash drawn from bank   —

                                                                     308.55

Deduct payments: Cash paid into bank   150.00
                  Cash Expenses per Cash Book   112.25   (262.25)

Cash in Till at end of week 27/3   33.30
Cash in Pocket at end of week 27/3   13.00

This presents a difficulty because no distinction can be made between that part of the cash in your pocket which belongs to the business and that part which belongs to you.

The easiest way out of this difficulty is not to show your own wages as a specific weekly payment in your Cash Book. You then treat all the cash remaining in your pocket at the end of each week as belonging to the business.

(Note that only business payments should be recorded in your Cash Book.)

You can then derive the amount of cash that you have used for private purposes during the week by working out the cash difference.

Example

Take the week ending 6/3 in our example. Figure 2 (pages 18–19) shows that £60.00 was drawn for private expenditure during that week.

If you did not keep your private cash separate from your business cash this entry would be missed out. Total cash payments for the week ending 6/3 would then be:

$$£196.25 - £60.00 = £136.25$$

If we assume that the entire £60.00 drawn was spent during the week then the cash in hand at the end of the week would still be £63 as shown in Figure 4.

Your Cash Control Account would now look like the example shown on page 33.

The problem with this method is that you lose the 'control' function of the Cash Control Account. You can no longer tell whether or not you have omitted a business cash payment because all cash differences are now assumed to be private expenses.

For this reason it is to be strongly recommended that you *draw a specific amount of cash each week for your personal expenditure.*

Keep this cash completely separate from your business cash. The methods illustrated in the worked example assume that this has been done. NB: The Inland Revenue would not consider the records to be complete if Drawings were not recorded, which could give rise to difficulties in settling your tax affairs.

Example of Cash Control Account (see page 32)

	£	£
Cash in Till at start of week		50.00
Add Receipts:		
Takings		209.25
Sundry		–
Cash drawn from bank		100.00
		359.25
Deduct Payments:		
Cash paid into bank	100.00	
Cash Expenses	136.25	236.25
		123.00
Deduct:		
Cash in Till at end of week		63.00
Difference: Personal Drawings		60.00

2. Note carefully that in arriving at £33.30 as the cash in the till on Friday evening 27/3 in Figure 3, we have taken out of the till £150.00 with the intention of banking this amount.

This would normally be paid into the bank on the day that it was taken out of the till, for security reasons.

In our example, however, we have assumed that the £150.00 was not banked until 2/4 (2 April) in order to illustrate the procedure for dealing with 'Amounts banked not on Statement' in Figure 5, Chapter 5.

3. *Simplification of the Cash Control Account.* If you always pay the whole of your Takings/Sales directly into your bank account without using any of the cash received to pay for expenses, that is you draw all cash needed to meet expenses from the bank, you can simplify the Cash Control Account as follows:

	£
Cash in Till/in hand at start of week	50.00
Add: Cash drawn from bank	209.25
	259.25
Deduct: Cash expenses per Cash Book	196.25
Cash in Till at end of week	63.00

The figures used in the above example are from the week ending 6/3 in Figures 2 and 3 of the previous chapters.

Note that all receipts, including any Sundry Receipts, must be paid directly into your bank account if this method is to be used.

Also note that the cash drawn from the bank to meet expenses has had to be increased from £100.00 to £209.25 because all the Takings are now banked intact. This will still leave £63.00 in the till at the end of the week.

4. *Use of Petty Cash box under the 'Imprest' system.* In order to use this method of controlling business cash expenditure, you must, as in point 3 above, pay all your receipts into the bank without using any part of them to pay expenses.

The next step is to obtain a Petty Cash box, preferably a metal one with a good lock.

You draw from the bank a specific sum of cash which you estimate will cover your business expenses for a suitable period, depending on how often you want to go to the bank.

This is your Imprest float which you keep in your cash box.

Every time you take money out of the box to pay for something, you put into the box a piece of paper (Petty Cash voucher) showing the amount that you have taken out and what it was for, or the actual receipt if you are able to obtain one.

Thus, at any time, the amount of money in the box plus the value of the receipts in the box should be equal to the Imprest float.

When the cash in the box runs low you draw from your bank the amount needed to restore the Imprest float to its original amount. Place that amount in the cash box and at the same time remove all the vouchers in the box. These can then be entered into your Cash Book as shown in Figure 2.

NB. If you use this method, there is no need to prepare a cash control account to ensure that you have recorded all business cash payments.

Chapter 5

How to Reconcile Your Cash Book with Your Bank Statements

This chapter can be ignored if you would prefer to leave the work to your accountant. However, the more the accountant does for you, the higher his or her charges will be.

The meaning of bank reconciliation

This is a technique which confuses many people but is really quite straightforward.

The aim of the bank reconciliation is to ensure that all transactions which pass through your bank account are correctly recorded in your Cash Book.

As the computer-produced bank statements are generally more accurate than hand-written Cash Books, it is possible to highlight errors in a Cash Book by comparing it with the entries on the bank statement.

When to prepare a bank reconciliation

You can reconcile your Cash Book with your bank statement at any time, be it daily, weekly, monthly or annually, provided that you have a copy of the bank statement which covers the relevant period.

It is advisable to prepare a bank reconciliation at least once a month for most businesses, however, because the longer the gap between reconciliations, the more entries there are to check.

How to prepare a bank reconciliation

The layout for a bank reconciliation is shown in Figure 6 (on page 38).

Stage 1

You must write up your Cash Book to the date at which you wish to prepare the reconciliation. In our example, we wish to prepare a bank reconciliation at the end of March.

Oxbridge Bank Ltd
2 Oxe Rd
Oxbridge

Account No: 12345687

Date: 3 April 198-

Figure 5. *Bank Statement*

Date		Payments £	Receipts £	Balance £
28/2	100105			
2/3	100109	20.00		
2/3	100107	30.00		
2/3	100108	25.00		2729.00
2/3	Sundry Receipt	7.00		
5/3	100112	100.00		2747.00
5/3	Standing Order	85.00	80.00	
6/3	100111	100.00		2562.00
6/3	100110	100.00		
6/3	Sundry Receipt		100.00	
6/3	100113	75.00		2462.00
7/3	100114	36.00		2387.00
9/3	100115	33.00		
9/3	100116	112.00		2318.00
11/3	100118	95.00		
11/3	100117			211.00

Date	Description	Payments	Receipts	Balance
13/3	Sundry Receipt		100.00	2131.00
14/3	100120	120.00		
14/3	100119	70.00		1941.00
15/3	302202	250.00		
15/3	302201	6.00		1685.00
16/3	302203	82.00		1603.00
18/3	302205	150.00		
18/3	302204	70.00		1383.00
20/3	302206	200.00		
20/3	Sundry Receipt		250.00	1433.00
23/3	302208	75.00		
23/3	302207	50.00		1308.00
24/3	302209	100.00		1208.00
25/3	302210	33.00		
25/3	302212	35.00		1140.00
26/3	302213	6.00		1134.00
27/3	Charges	3.50		
27/3	Interest	17.00		1113.50
2/4	Sundry Receipt		150.00	1263.50
3/4	302214	25.00		
3/4	302215	95.00		1143.50

Note

We wish to ascertain the balance of funds available for use at 31/3. This date lies between 27/3 and 2/4 on the Bank Statement. If we draw a line across the statement after 27/3, the last balance above that line, ie £1,113.50, is the figure to be used in reconciling the balance shown by the bank statement to that shown by the Cash Book.

Figure 6. *Bank Account Summary*

	£
Balance per last Summary at 28/2	2,747.00
Paid into bank in last 4 weeks	600.00
Bank Payments Summary	(2,203.50)
Balance per Cash Book carried forward	£1,143.50

Reconciliation of Bank Account

	£	£
Balance shown by Bank Statement at 31/3		1,113.50
Deduct: Unpresented cheques:		
Cheque No 302215	95.00	
302214	25.00	
		(120.00)
Add: Amounts banked not on statement		150.00
Balance per Cash Book as shown by Bank Account Summary above		£1,143.50

Notes

Unpresented cheques: These are cheques which were written out and sent to your supplier before the end of the period concerned (in this case 31/3), which have not yet been presented to your bank for payment and therefore do not appear on your Bank Statement.

Amounts banked not on Statement: In this example, £150 was recorded as banked in the Cash Book on Friday 27/3 and was removed from the till on that date, but was not actually banked until Thursday 2/4.

The important point to note is that it is not the balance shown by your Bank Statement at 31/3 which necessarily shows the actual money available to you at that date. Rather it is the balance as shown by your Bank Account Summary (which summarises your Cash Book) that shows the amount of money still available for use.

We have therefore written into our Cash Book all cheques dated up to 31/3, all standing orders paid in March, all non-cheque items which appear on our statement up to 31/3, and all receipts removed from our till ready for banking, prior to the 31st March.

Stage 2

Take your statement, shown in Figure 5 (on pages 36–37), which must show all items presented to the bank before 31/3 in our example and preferably also show some of the items presented after that date.

Draw a line with a ruler and pen straight across the statement underneath the date on the statement at which you wish to reconcile your account.

In our example in Figure 5, we wish to reconcile our account at 31/3, which lies between 27/3 and 2/4 as shown by the statement. Therefore, the statement balance at the 31st March was the same as at 27/3, because no further items were processed by the bank between 27/3 and 2/4.

Our line is drawn underneath 27/3 and the statement balance to be used in the reconciliation is £1,113.50.

Stage 3

Prepare a Bank Account Summary from the information in the Cash Book. In our example we have:

Total amount banked in March, per Figure 3 (pages 24–25)	£600.00
Total bank payments in March, per Figure 1 (pages 12–13)	£2,203.50

The balance that we started with at the beginning of March comes from our last bank reconciliation.

If you have not prepared a bank reconciliation before, however, then you must prepare a partial one for the beginning of the month.

As this can be a little tricky, we have shown the detailed instructions on how to do this on pages 41–43.

For now we shall assume that we had prepared a bank reconciliation at the end of February and therefore that we know the balance at 28/2 to be £2,747.00.

Thus the balance in our Cash Book at 31/3 is arrived at by adding the March receipts to the opening balance and deducting the March payments.

(If the balance brought forward at 28/2 had been an overdraft, you would add the March payments to it and deduct the March receipts, because payments make an overdraft worse while receipts improve it.)

Stage 4

To reconcile the balance obtained above to the balance shown by the Bank Statement at 31/3 and thereby prove the Cash Book information

to be correct, do the calculation shown in Figure 6, Reconciliation o
Bank Account (page 38).

To identify 'unpresented cheques' and 'amounts banked not or
statement', use a coloured pen and tick each item on the Statement an
each corresponding item in your Cash Book up to the line that you hav
drawn across your statement. Do not tick any items below that line.

When you have done this, look at your Cash Book and make a list o
any items that have not been ticked, adding them up to obtain a total
Unticked cheques are 'unpresented cheques'. Unticked receipts banked
are 'amounts banked not on statement'.

Warning in the event of an overdraft
The example shown in Figure 6 assumes that we have some money in the
bank at 31/3.

If instead we had an overdraft at this date, the adjustments that mus
be made to the statement balance to equate with the Cash Book balance
are reversed:

Suppose that the statement showed an overdraft of £30.00, that we had
unpresented cheques of £250.00, and that we had amounts banked no
on statement of £350.00.

The bank reconciliation is calculated as follows:

		£	
Balance per Statement at 31/3		30.00	(Overdrawn)
Add: Unpresented cheques		250.00	
		280.00	
Deduct:	Amounts banked not on Statement	350.00	
Balance per Cash Book at 31/3		£70.00	(Positive)

In this situation the unpresented cheques have the effect of increasing
your overdraft, while the amounts banked not on statement will reduce
your overdraft. In this example the £350.00 receipt not only wipes ou
the overdraft, but leaves £70.00 in the Bank Account available for use

Main causes of failure to reconcile a bank balance to a Cash Book balance

1. All items on the Statement have not been recorded in the Cash
   Book.
2. The wrong figures have been recorded in the Cash Book because

the cheque stub or receipt counterfoil has been written out incorrectly.

3. Transposition errors in the Cash Book, ie you wrote £36 when you meant £63.

4. Unpresented cheques in the previous reconciliation are still unpresented at the date of the next reconciliation and you have not included them with this month's list of unpresented cheques.

5. Addition errors in the Total column of the Payments Cash Book, or the Amount Banked column of the Receipts Cash Book.

Appendix

Methods of finding the opening Cash Book balance where you have not previously prepared a bank reconciliation are given below. Choose one of the four following sets of instructions which suits your circumstances:

1. *If you have been in business for some time and have been keeping a Cash Book*

  (a) Draw a line across your Bank Statement underneath the last date in the previous month to the one in which you are preparing your reconciliation. In Figure 5 (pages 36–37), this line would be drawn under 28/2 and the balance to be used would be £2,729.00.

  (b) Compare your Cash Book payments in February with your March Bank Statement. Make a list of any February cheques in the Cash Book which are not on the Statement until after 28/2.

  (c) Compare your Cash Book amounts banked in February with your March Statement and list any items in the February Cash Book which are not on the Statement until after 28/2.

  (d) Do the following calculation with the information obtained above:

		£	£
Balance per Statement at 28/2			2,729.00
Add: February bankings on Statement in March			80.00
			2,809.00
Deduct: February cheques on Statement in March	100109	30.00	
	100107	25.00	
	100108	7.00	62.00
Opening Cash Book Balance at 1/3			£2,747.00

2. If you have been in business for some time but have not kept a Cash Book

Follow the instructions given above, but use your February cheque stubs and paying-in book counterfoils for comparison with your March Bank Statement, instead of your Cash Book.

Example

Assume that our business started on 16/2:

Bank Statement

Date	No	Paid £	Rec'd £	Balance £	
10/2	100995	30		1,000	
11/2	997	20		980	
15/2	Sundry		100	1,080	←Balance per —
16/2	990	50		1,030	Statement at
17/2	999	30		1,000	start
18/2	Sundry		150	1,150	
20/2	101001	50 —		1,100	

6/2 Fred £50.00 100990	14/2 Jim £30.00 100999	17/2 Tom £50.00 101001	Cash Received on the 15/2

Unpresented Cheques at the 15/2

First Cheque after date on which business started

COMPUTE OPENING CASH BOOK BALANCE:

Balance per Statement at the 15/2		£1,080 ← — —
Less: Unpresented Cheques	£50	
	£30	
		£80
		£1,000
Add: Outstanding Receipt		£150 ← — —
Cash Book Bank Balance at start of Business		£1,150

3. *If you are newly started in business and intend to operate your business through your private bank account*

    (a) Take the balance shown by your statement at the date on which you start to make business payments, or pay in business receipts.

    (b) Deduct from that amount any payments which were made before that date, which appear on the statement after that date.

    (c) Add on any amounts which were received before that date, which were not banked until after that date.

    (d) The result is your opening Cash Book balance.

NB. If your bank balance is an overdraft you must add items (b) and deduct items (c).

4. *If you are newly started in business and open a new bank account*

The opening Cash Book balance is zero.

Chapter 6

Quick Reference to Specific Problems

Chapters 1, 2 and 3 have shown how to use a columnar Cash Book record all business receipts and payments in such a way as to prese: essential information in an orderly and easily understood manner.

In Figures 1, 2 and 3 we have indicated the way in which some of th more common receipts and payments can be recorded. It is not possib to illustrate every conceivable recording entry that you may need make in the course of your particular business, but the guidelines give should be sufficient to point you in the right direction.

The following notes are intended to be used as a quick reference to th treatment of some of the less obvious problems that you may be face with from time to time.

1. Sundry Receipts

Any receipts of funds into your business which do not arise in you normal course of trade should be recorded in the Sundry Receip column of your Cash Book.

Some of the more common items that would fall in this category ar

Insurance refunds/compensation
Income Tax refunds
VAT refunds
Proceeds from the sale of your assets – cars and equipment
Government or local authority grants.

2. Personal Drawings

In addition to the cash that you draw from the business for your ow living expenses, ie your wages, the following payments are also to b treated as Drawings:

(a) Income Tax on your profits from the business (but not Pay As Yo Earn – PAYE – on the wages that you pay to your employees, ▪ SC60 tax which you deduct from payments to your subcontra tors if you operate a business in the building industry. Suc payments can be shown in the Wages column of your Cash Book

(b) Your own National Insurance contributions.
(c) Any private purchases or expenses that you pay for with business money, rather than using the money which you have specifically drawn as your wages.

3. Purchase of Assets on hire purchase

If you buy an asset for use in your business on HP the amounts to be shown in your Cash Book are:

(a) The initial deposit paid
(b) Each instalment as it arises.

All these payments should be shown in a column for HP payments or, as in Figure 1 (pages 12–13), a column for bank Standing Order charges if you pay the instalments by standing order.

NB. The actual cost of the asset purchased, as shown by the invoice, is not recorded in the Cash Book.

You should file your invoice with a copy of the HP Agreement instead of allocating it a number and filing it in the normal way. Your accountant will make the necessary adjustments when he prepares your accounts.

4. Capital items

Capital items are items such as vans, cars, furniture, machinery, tools and equipment which are used in the course of your business.

The taxation treatment of such items is different from everyday revenue expenses such as electricity, telephone, rent and so on and for this reason each item of capital expenditure needs to be identified separately in your Cash Book.

There can sometimes be difficulties in deciding whether a payment is for a capital item or a revenue item. For instance, in the case of tools, small tools are often treated as a trading expense (ie a revenue item) particularly if they require regular replacement. As a general rule, small items that are regularly replaced can be shown in a column headed 'Loose Tools' and all other capital items of equipment should be shown in the column headed 'Capital Items'.

5. Repayment of loans

If you borrow money for use in your business from any source you should record the receipt of the loan in your Sundry Receipts column and show the repayments in a separate column of your payments Cash Book. If the repayments are made infrequently, however, instead of wasting a column, record the repayments in the Sundry Expenses column and label them as 'loan repayments'.

Your accountant will make the necessary adjustments at the end of the year. If you have to pay interest on the loan, make sure that you have some form of document to show how much interest is being charged.

Interest on loans used in the futherance of your business is usually a tax allowable expense.

6. Payments by credit card (Barclaycard, Access etc)

When paying for goods or expenses by credit card, the payment that you will record in your Cash Book will be the cheque payment to the credit card company.

For the purposes of your annual accounts, however, your accountant needs to know the nature of the items paid for with your credit card.

Example
Suppose that you receive your credit card statement for the month of March, which shows the following details:

Statement	£
Balance brought forward from previous statement	130.00
Payment received	100.00
	30.00
Interest charge	2.50
	32.50
2/3 ABC Service Station	10.00
7/3 D&E Cash 'n' Carry	30.00
15/3 ABC Service Station	15.00
16/3 Beta Department Store	65.00
Balance due at 31/3	£152.50

You decide to pay the credit card company £100.00 and you make out the cheque on 5/4. The details to be recorded in your Cash Book are:

Date	Supplier (name)	Invoice number	Cheque number	Total amount £
5/4	Credit Card Co		201112	100.00

This entry records the details on the cheque stub. The problem remaining is to record in the correct analysis columns the individual components which make up the payment of £100.00.

To do this we must assume that the £100.00 is applied to pay off the items on the statement in the order in which they appear.

Suppose that the details given by your receipts for the items on your statement are as follows:

(a) Balance brought forward £30.00 Goods for Resale (ie Purchases) dated 27/2.
(b) 2/3 to ABC Service Station £10.00 for petrol.
(c) 7/3 to D&E Cash 'n' Carry (Stationers) £30.00 for writing paper, envelopes etc.
(d) 15/3 to ABC Service Station £15.00 for petrol.
(e) 16/3 to Beta Department Store £65.00 for a coffee table for your home.

We will assume that the number you gave to the previous cheque payment in your Cash Book was 18.

We have five receipts relating to a single cheque payment of £100.00. You would number these receipts 19, 20, 21, 22, 23 in the order in which they appear on the statement.

The layout of the analysis columns in your cheque payments Cash Book would be as follows:

Invoice number	Cheque number	Total amount £	Purchases £	Motor expenses £	Print & Stat £	Personal drawings £	Sundry expenses £
19.23*	201112	100.00	30.00 (a)	25.00 (b)(d)	30.00 (c)	12.50 (e)	2.50

If in the following month you bought nothing more with your credit card, but were charged £1.50 interest and you paid off the whole balance outstanding at the end of the month, the Cash Book entries would be:

Invoice number	Cheque number	Total amount £	Personal drawings £	Sundry expenses £
23*	201128	54.00	52.50	1.50

Points to note

1. The last item on the statement, to which we have given the reference number 23, is partially paid by the first cheque of £100.00, the balance of £52.50 being paid as part of the cheque for £54.00 on receipt of the following month's statement.
2. When the cheque for £54.00 is paid, the invoice reference number to be used is 23 which was, of course, also used for the previous

month's payment. The reference number is marked with an asterisk (*) in order to show that the one invoice relates to two payments.

3. Credit card interest charges are not an allowable expense for tax purposes at this time, but they must still be shown in the Sundry Expenses column in order to balance the Cash Book. Your accountant will make the necessary year-end adjustment for tax purposes.

Chapter 7
How to Use Pre-printed Cash Books

The earlier chapters explained how to set about laying out a columnar Cash Book from scratch.

For small businesses and self-employed people who have only a small number of receipts and payments to record each week, there are a number of excellent pre-printed Cash Books available from most stationers which can considerably reduce the amount of work involved in producing adequate business records.

The main limitation to these Cash Books is the number of items that can be recorded each week. Before buying one of them, count the number of lines on one page available for recording payments for goods. This will give you an idea of whether or not the book will be suitable for you.

If you begin to use this type of book but find that you cannot squeeze all your receipts and payments for a week into the space allotted, then it is not really suitable.

You could, of course, buy two or more of these books and enter each week's items on more than one page. However, it may be cheaper to go for the large columnar Cash Book from the beginning which has the advantage that no space need be wasted.

Basic layout of the Cash Book

There are a number of makes of this type of book, but they all follow the same basic principles. Our example in Figure 7 on pages 50 and 51 follows the basic layout of the Simplex Cash Book from which we can illustrate the relationship of the various sections of the Cash Book to each other. The same points are relevant to all other Cash Books.

1. Each page is intended to cover all receipts and payments for one week. There are usually 53 pages per book to cover a 53-week period.
2. Each page is laid out to record:
    (a) each day's receipts and amounts paid into the bank
    (b) payments for goods   } with separate colums
    (c) payments for expenses } for cash/cheques

Figure 7. *Example of pre-printed Cash Book page*

Week commencing.......

Receipts

Date	Takings £	Sundry items £	Sundry details	Bankings £
2/3 3/3 4/3 5/3 6/3	45.00 40.00 55.00 64.00 90.00	85.00	Income tax refund	225.00 100.00
	294.00	85.00		325.00

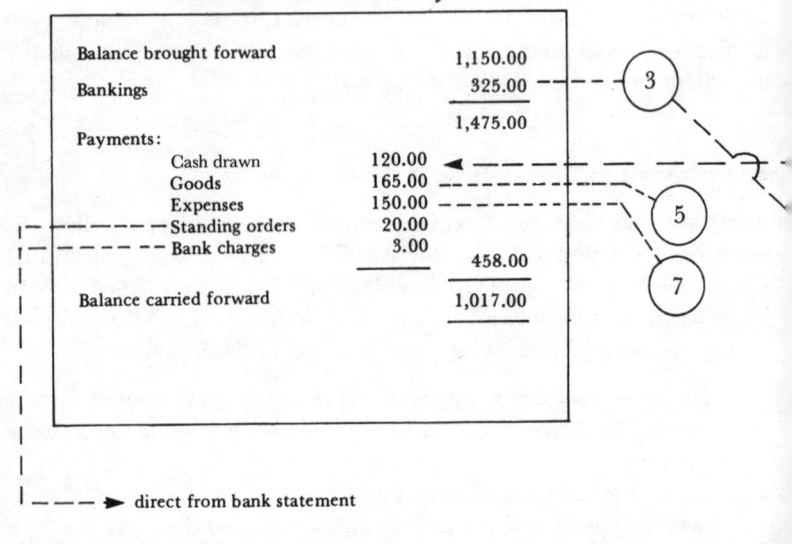

Bank account summary

Balance brought forward		1,150.00
Bankings		325.00
		1,475.00
Payments:		
Cash drawn	120.00	
Goods	165.00	
Expenses	150.00	
Standing orders	20.00	
Bank charges	3.00	
		458.00
Balance carried forward		1,017.00

- - - ► direct from bank statement

Payments

Payments for goods

Date	Supplier	Cash £	Cheque £
2/3	A Ltd		25.00
2/3	Mr B	5.00	
2/3	Mr C	8.00	
3/3	D Ltd	10.00	
4/3	E Ltd		75.00
4/3	Mrs F		30.00
5/3	G Partners		35.00
		23.00	165.00

④ ⑤

Payments for expenses

Expense	Cash £	Cheque £
Rent	5.00	
Rates		20.00
Motor expenses	15.00	
Insurance		35.00
Telephone		
Cleaning		
Tools		
Light and heat		65.00
Sundry expenses	6.00	
Wife's wages	10.00	
Other wages		
Drawings	60.00	
Capital items		30.00
	96.00	150.00

⑥ ⑦

Cash account summary

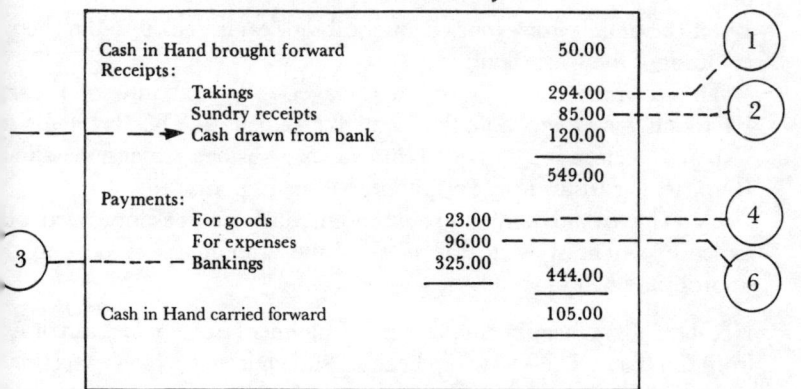

```
Cash in Hand brought forward              50.00        ①
Receipts:
        Takings                          294.00 ------
        Sundry receipts                   85.00 ------  ②
        Cash drawn from bank             120.00
                                         ------
                                         549.00
Payments:
        For goods                23.00 ------------ ④
        For expenses             96.00 ------
        Bankings                325.00 -------
                                       ------  444.00   ⑥
Cash in Hand carried forward             105.00
```

③

51

     (d) a summary of each week's Cash Account

     (e) A summary of each week's Bank Account.

3. At the back of the book there are summaries for all of the week entries so that an overall position for the year can be obtaine There is also some provision for dealing with VAT, but th methods used differ considerably from book to book. Th principles remain the same as discussed in Chapter 8.

How to use the Cash Book

Stage 1

Receipts from customers should be written into the appropriate slot i the Takings column daily.

Stage 2

Sundry receipts (those not arising directly from your normal course business) are recorded in the Sundry Receipt column and a note mae of the source of the receipt next to the appropriate figure.

Stage 3

When you go to your bank to pay money into your account, you recor the amount deposited in the Bankings column. This amount should the same as the total shown on the paying-in slip.

Stage 4

Enter the details from your cheque stubs for each week into the chequ columns of the Cash Book.

The payments section on each page is divided into two part Payments for Goods and Payments for Expenses. The Payments f Expenses section is subdivided into various business expense heading Rent, Rates, Insurance, Telephone, Motor Expenses etc.

If you have paid more than one amount during a week for a particul: expense you must write the total of the amounts paid next to th appropriate heading.

NB. There is no heading in the expense payments section for cash draw from the bank. The Drawings heading shown in the Expenses section your own wages or personal expenses paid with business money, whic is something quite different.

Stage 5

You record cash drawn from the bank by adding up from the chequ stubs the total cash drawn during the week. This amount is entered the Bank Account Summary under the heading Cash Drawn and in the Cash Account Summary as a receipt under the heading Cash Drawn from Bank.

Stage 6
Enter your cash payments into the Cash Book from your cash receipts (invoices), together with any other cash payment that you have made for which you have no receipt.

Stage 7
Examine your bank statement when you receive it and enter the total of any standing order payments or other non-cheque payments, such as bank charges, into the Cash Book.

The Simplex Cash Book has a space for such payments in the Bank Account Summary. An alternative way of recording them would be to ignore the boxes in the Summary and record the payments as Sundry payments in the Expenses section on each page. This method has the advantage that the standing order payments would then appear in the Annual Summary at the back of the Cash Book.

These items should appear in the week in which they were actually paid by the bank; otherwise the balance per the Bank Account Summary for that week will not show the true balance.

In practice it is usually easier to enter them on the most recent page so as to avoid having to alter all of the brought-forward totals from the previous weeks' Summaries which you have already completed. The balance shown on the most recent page should then show the true position.

If you know that a standing order will pass through your account on a certain date, remember to enter it into your Cash Book at the appropriate time to avoid this minor discrepancy.

Stage 8
Add up each column and write the totals in the spaces provided.

Stage 9
Write each column total in the appropriate space in the Bank and Cash Account Summaries. In Figure 7 we have referenced each column to the appropriate spot in the Summaries so that the necessary entries can be easily identified.

NB. Each column total is entered only once into one or other of the two Summaries, with the exception of column 3 which belongs in both Bank

and Cash Account Summaries. This is because Bankings are paid out o
the Cash Account into the Bank Account.

Stage 10
Bring forward the closing balances from the Cash and Bank Accoun
Summaries on the previous page and record these amounts in the space
provided.

Stage 11
Add up the Bank Account Summary and the Cash Account Summar
to obtain the closing balances on the two accounts. These will be carrie
forward to the next page.

Stage 12
The method for reconciling your bank account balance as shown b
your Cash Book with that shown by your bank statement is as describe
in Chapter 5.

If you are unable to follow this, however, do not worry about it. You
accountant will sort it out at the end of your financial year, although i
will help you to keep tight control over your business if you can maste
the principles involved.

Stage 13: filing invoices
Sales invoices. If you give your customer an invoice, you should keep
carbon copy for yourself and file it in numerical order if your invoices are
numbered sequentially, or otherwise in date order.

Purchase/Expense invoices. It is usually difficult to file invoices in numerica
order when using this type of Cash Book, as no specific space is allowe
for a reference number.

Generally, the easiest way of filing your receipts is to clip each week'
receipts together and put them in an envelope marked with the wee
number, or date to which they relate.

Stage 14
Fill in the Summaries at the back of the book with the current week'
details. There will usually be summaries for:

Takings/Sales
Sundry Receipts
Payments for Goods
Payments for Expenses with a separate column for each major
type of expense

Personal Drawings
Capital items bought.

It is not advisable to prepare your own accounts for submission to the Inland Revenue even though this type of book does give additional summaries to enable you to do so. You would normally be better off employing an accountant to prepare your year-end accounts from your books and to handle your tax affairs, as the complexities of the tax system are perhaps best dealt with between two people who speak the same professional language. Completing the Summaries listed above, therefore, is usually all that is necessary.

Main points to watch when using a pre-printed Cash Book

1. 'Cash Drawn from the Bank' is often confused with 'Drawings'. Beware of this. 'Drawings' appear in the Expenses payments section of the Cash Book. This is the amount that you draw from the business for your own personal use, that is, your wages.

   'Cash Drawn from the Bank' is the amount that you take out of the bank in cash in order to pay for your cash expenses. This is shown in the Bank Summary Account and the Cash Summary Account. It is not an 'expense'.

2. 'Drawings' and 'Capital Items' are usually shown in their own separate Summaries at the back of the Cash Book even though they are recorded each week in the Expenses payments section of each page in the Cash Book.

3. If you use business money to pay for personal expenses (rather than using the cash that you have drawn for your wages), you must record these payments as 'Drawings' along with the wages that you have drawn for yourself.

4. In order to keep tight control over your business cash expenditure you should ensure that you do not mix up business cash with the cash that you have drawn for your own wages. Do not use cash from your wages to pay for business expenses.

5. The actual business cash left over at the end of the week should be the same as the balance of cash in hand shown by the Cash Account Summary in the Cash Book.

   If actual cash in hand is greater than that shown in the Cash Book, then you have probably omitted a receipt from your Sales/ Takings column.

   If actual cash in hand is less than that shown in the Cash Book then you have probably omitted a business cash payment from the Cash Book.

Before jumping to either of these conclusions, however, alway check:

(a) The addition of all the cash columns, including the Taking column.
(b) That you have brought forward the correct cash in hand from the previous page.
(c) That you have correctly added up the Cash Summar Account.
(d) That you have not made a transposition error in any of th cash columns, such as writing £56, for instance, when yo meant £65.

6. You will find among the Summaries at the back of the Cash Boc one for 'Goods Taken for Own Consumption'. This should only b used if you take goods for your own use out of business stock. Fc instance, if you are a butcher you might take the family mea supply out of your shop. If you do not pay the full market price fc this into your till, then you should record the cost to the busine (the amount that the business paid for the stock) in the Summar of 'Goods Taken for Own Consumption'.

If you pay the full market price for the goods that you have take for your own use and record this amount as a sale in your Cas Book, there is no need to make use of the 'Goods Taken for Ow Consumption' summary.

Chapter 8

How to Prepare VAT Records and Complete a VAT Return

The law relating to Value Added Tax is complicated, but fortunately it is not necessary for most traders to know the ins and outs of all of it.

This chapter indicates the main problems to be overcome in order to be able to complete a VAT Return.

The VAT Return is a form which is sent out to all VAT registered traders at three-monthly intervals on which the trader has to show how much tax he owes to the Customs & Excise who are responsible for administering the tax.

Customs & Excise officers make regular visits to traders who are VAT registered to answer their queries and to check that the trader is calculating the tax correctly.

The first hurdle to overcome is deciding whether or not you should be VAT registerd to start with.

Should I be registered for VAT?

This depends on how high your turnover (Sales) is expected to be in each 12-month period.

The level to which sales may rise before VAT registration becomes necessary is determined by the Chancellor of the Exchequer at each Budget and usually applies from the start of each fiscal year (6 April), or a date specified in the Budget.

For the current year, 1989/90, the following applies:

1. If you expect your sales to exceed £23,600 in the 12 months to your next accounting year-end, then you must apply for VAT registration from 21 days after you had reasonable grounds for that expectation.

2. If your sales exceed £8,000 in any calendar quarter, that is January-March, April-June etc, you must register for VAT from 21 days after the end of the quarter in which those results arise.

If you are at all unsure as to whether you should be registered or not, you can always ring or write to any local Customs & Excise VAT Office and they will advise you what to do.

As well as the above constraints, some businesses do not need to register even if they exceed the turnover limits because VAT is not always charged on all goods and services.

In some cases, VAT registration may be allowed to a trader, even though his sales do not reach the limits, if he can show that his business will suffer if he is not registered. If in doubt, always contact your local VAT Office.

Your VAT registration number

Assuming that you are liable to register for VAT and that you have notified the Customs & Excise accordingly on Form VAT 1 (which you will obtain from any VAT Office or from your accountant), you will be sent a certificate of registration with your VAT number on it and the date from which you are VAT registered.

You must not charge VAT on your goods and services before the registration date. Similarly, you may not recover VAT charged to you by other traders prior to your VAT registration date, except for the VAT charged on goods which you already had in stock at that date and which you will be selling to customers with VAT included.

It is therefore a good idea to take stock on the date on which you become VAT registered.

After the registration date, you must show your VAT number on your sales invoices, and the amount of VAT charged should normally be shown as a separate item.

You may not claim input tax (explained below) relief on goods and services that you purchase unless the invoice shows a VAT number.

Record keeping

The records that you must keep and which will be required for inspection by the Customs & Excise should be designed to enable you to identify the following:

1. *Output tax*

Output tax is the VAT that you charge your customer when you make a sale.

This VAT is the amount that you are liable to pay over to the Customs & Excise (subject to what follows).

It is important to note that the date on which you become liable to pay the tax (the tax point), is normally the date on which the goods change ands, which may not necessarily be the same date that you receive ayment from your customer.

If your turnover is below certain limits (currently £250,000) you may e eligible to apply to the Customs & Excise to account for VAT on the ash that you receive in the VAT quarter rather than on the sales voiced in that quarter.

This is known as the 'Cash Accounting Scheme' and may be useful to usinesses where cash flow needs to be carefully regulated.

Input tax

nput tax is the VAT that you have to pay your supplier when you buy oods from him and which would normally be shown on his invoices to ou.

You may claim this tax back from Customs & Excise when you omplete the VAT Return. Thus you only pay over to Customs & Excise ie net output tax after deducting the input tax from the total output tax i any VAT period.

Iow to record VAT transactions if you are VAT registered

ales (based on Methods 1 or 2 of Chapter 3)

f the goods and services which you sell are subject to standard rate VAT ou must add to your normal selling price the standard rate of VAT in orce at the time of sale (currently 15 per cent). This is the output tax.

xample

uppose you sell something for £100. If you are VAT registered you must dd on £15 (15 per cent of £100) and charge your customer £115. Of this, 100 belongs to you and £15 belongs to the Customs & Excise.

To record this transaction, you need to alter the column headings of our Cash Received Book slightly:

ate	Customer (name)	Invoice number	Sales net	VAT	Sales gross	Sundry receipts	Amount banked
			£	£	£	£	£
/3	Fred	12	100.00	15.00	115.00	–	115.00

ales (based on Methods 3 or 4 where you do not have individual invoices or each customer)

ou must ensure that when you price your goods, you allow for the 15 er cent VAT on top of your normal mark-up.

Example

Purchase cost	£80	(excluding VAT
Plus Mark-up (say) 25%	£20	
(to give Gross Profit 20%)	£100	
Plus VAT 15%	£15	
Selling Price	£115	

Most electronic tills will calculate the VAT for you. However, if you not have one of these machines, you can calculate the VAT on your Sa as follows:

Date	Amount in till at start	Amount in till at end	Sundry receipts	Amount banked	Takin
	£	£	£	£	£
3/3	50.00	65.00	–	100.00	115.0

$$£115 \times \frac{\text{VAT Rate}}{100 + \text{VAT Rate}}$$

VAT Rate 15 per cent:

$$£115 \times \frac{15}{115} = £15 \text{ or}$$

$$£115 \times \frac{3}{23} = £15$$

The calculations shown above assume that all of your sales are standa rated for VAT purposes.

If some of your sales are zero rated or exempt, you will need to use o of the scheme calculations for working out output tax on your sales. T is discussed in some detail later on.

You can find out which category your sales come under by asking a copy of VAT Notice 701 'Scope and Coverage' at your local VA Office. If in doubt, ask the VAT Office direct.

Payments on VAT supplies

There are basically two alternative ways of recording VAT on yo purchases/expenses. Which method to use depends upon the length time you normally wait before paying your suppliers.

Method 1

Use this where you pay most of your bills immediately.

By adding an extra column to your analysed Cash Book you can very simply account for all of the VAT on your payments (input tax).

The headings for Figure 1 in Chapter 1 (pages 12–13) become:

Date	Supplier	Invoice number	Cheque number	Total amount	VAT	Cash	Purchases
				£	£	£	£

For instance, let us say that you pay the following invoice as soon as you receive the goods on the 3rd March:

Fred		
VAT No: XXX	Invoice No: 1053	
	Date: 3/3	
Goods	£100.00	
VAT 15%	£15.00	
Amount due	£115.00	

You pay by cheque so that the entry is:

Date	Supplier	Invoice number	Cheque number	Total amount	VAT	Purchases
				£	£	£
3/3	Fred	6	100233	115.00	15.00	100.00

Points to note

1. You can only claim VAT back if your supplier is VAT registered. You can tell this by whether his VAT registration number is shown on the invoice.
2. The date of the entry in your Cash Book must be the date that you make out the cheque, which may not be the same date as the invoice.
3. The ringed number 6 on the invoice in the example is the number that you have given to the invoice before you file it with your other paid invoices.
4. The tax point date is usually, but not always, the same as the invoice date. The tax point is generally determined by the date on which goods or services change hands.

Method 2

Use this where you make full use of any credit terms offered to you.

You may claim the input tax generally at the date shown as the ta point, which can be some time before you actually pay for the goods.

Since you normally pay VAT over to the Customs & Excise ever three months, you need to have a separate record of all the VAT that yo can claim back in order to be able to claim it at the earliest possibl opportunity.

You can achieve this by keeping a book with your purchase/expense invoices listed as you receive them, in tax point date order.

You should lay out the book as follows:

Date	Supplier (name)	Invoice number	Total amount £	VAT £	Standard rate net £	Zero £	Exempt £

The entry for our previous example would be:

3/3	Fred	6	£115.00	15.00	100.00		

Points to note

1. This book is not a Cash Book. It is designed purely to give you th information that you require to complete a VAT Return a outlined in Figure 11 to this chapter (page 72).
2. The referencing system that you use is slightly different from tha previously explained:

   (a) You should give each invoice a number as soon as you receiv it.
   (b) Make the entries in your VAT Register as shown above from the details on the invoice.
   (c) File the invoices in numerical order in a file labelled 'Unpaic Invoices'.
   (d) When you pay the amount outstanding, remove the invoic from this file and record the details in your Cash Book.

   NB. The number that you have given is the number that you ente in the Invoice Number column of the Cash Book. As you will no necessarily pay the invoices in the order in which they wer received, the numerical sequence in the Cash Book will be broken

   (e) When you have paid each invoice, file it in numerical sequenc in another file labelled 'Paid Invoices', so that the Customs & Excise inspectors can easily find the invoice relevant to each entry in the VAT Register.

The inspectors will call on you periodically to ensure that you are correctly accounting for VAT.

3. You can either record the payments in your Cash Book inclusive of VAT or you can insert an extra column for the VAT element in the payment as shown on page 61.

The latter method is to be preferred; each expense column will show the VAT-exclusive cost to you, which is the true cost to you, because the VAT that you are charged by your suppliers is offset against the VAT that you charge your customers.

If you use the slightly simpler first method, your accountant will make the necessary VAT adjustments at the end of your financial year.

If you are using one of the retail schemes as discussed later, the layout of the Purchase Invoice Register will depend upon the scheme that you decide to use.

Cash or credit sales

If all your sales are liable to standard rate VAT and you do not give or take credit, so that the date on which the goods change hands is also the payment date, then you can obtain the necessary VAT figures to complete the VAT Return direct from the VAT columns in your Cash Book. These columns can be inserted as follows:

Payments by Cheque (as per Chapter 1):

Date	Supplier (name)	Invoice number	Cheque number	Total amount	VAT	Cash drawn

Payments by Cash (as per Chapter 2):

Date	Supplier (name)	Invoice number	Total amount	VAT

Methods of recording income (as per Chapter 3):

Method 1

Date	Customer (name)	Invoice number	VAT	Sales/ Takings amount	Sundry receipts	Banked

Method 2

Date	Customer (name)	Invoice number	VAT	Sales/ Takings	Sundry receipts	Cash used for expenses	Banked

Note that the VAT figures in the Cash Received Book are *memo* figure only. That is, they are ignored for the purposes of balancing the Cash Book because the Sales/Takings column is the total amount received including the VAT.

In the Cash Paid Book and Cheques Paid Book the idea is to separate the VAT element of the payment from the item being analysed. For instance, if you bought some goods for cash that you intended to resell for £115.00 including 15 per cent VAT you would record the payment in your Cash Book as follows:

Date	Supplier (name)	Invoice number	Total amount £	VAT £	Goods for resale £
2/3	Fred	5	115.00	15.00	100.00

If there is a delay between the time that the goods change hands and the time that payment is made then you will have to keep a separate VAT book in addition to your Cash Book.

Gross Takings/Sales

In all cases the first thing to do is to identify taxable gross takings.

This is normally the total value of goods and services supplied by you in a VAT period as shown by your sales invoices. If you are using one of the retail schemes, however, gross takings can be calculated in one of two ways:

1. Standard method
The total cash received from business supplies in a VAT period, ignoring sales on credit, or

2. Optional method
The total cash received plus amounts owed by customers for goods supplied in the VAT period.

You can choose which method to use but must inform Customs & Excise if you use method 2.

You must add to the above total of sales the cost of goods including VAT that you have taken for your own personal use.

From this total is deducted any refunds for goods returned by customers.

Also, if you are using a retail scheme and receive business supplies in lieu of payment for goods and services that you supply, you must add the normal selling price including VAT of those supplies to your gross takings.

3. Amounts received for standard and zero rated supplies should be after deducting any cash discounts given and after deducting any returnable deposits.

VAT should be charged on non-returnable deposits as the money is received. You should not wait for the balance of the money to be paid before you account for the VAT on the deposit.

If you give your customer a discount provided that he does something for you in the future, then the gross takings on which VAT is worked out must exclude the discount. If the condition is later fulfilled you may issue a credit note to adjust for the additional amount charged on the first transaction.

If you allow a customer to pay by instalments, the sale value on which VAT is calculated must be the amount that he actually pays.

Sales to a specific customer

Where it is possible to identify sales to a specific customer, it is normal to issue a sales invoice to your customer which must show various details and may contain other details for your own accounting convenience.

Figure 8 (rounded to the nearest pound) on page 66 shows the information that must be shown on a sales invoice.

Usually the invoices would be numbered in sequence though it is not really necessary to do so.

Figure 9 on page 67 shows how to keep a record of the sales invoices for VAT purposes which should be kept in tax point date order.

Sales which cannot be identified with an individual customer

This is usually the case where the trader is a shopkeeper selling a wide variety of small items and where it is not practical to raise an individual invoice for each customer.

A problem then arises because all goods and services sold are not necessarily charged at the same rate of VAT. So, from your total gross takings, how do you know how much of the total includes VAT?

First, it should be pointed out that there are currently two rates of tax in Great Britain: standard rate = 15 per cent, and zero rate = 0 per cent.

Figure 8. *Sales invoice*

SALES INVOICE

Your Business Name Fred Bloggs & Co (Ltd — only if a
limited company)

Your Business Address 12 High St, Newtown

Your VAT Registration Number 000 3645 897

Your Customer's Name & Address

Percy & Co
23 Low St
Oldtown   Invoice No. 1000

                                          Tax point: 23/7/85

	£
(It is usual to give a description of the goods being sold)	111.00
Less 10% discount	11.00
Net Selling Price (rounded price)	
Plus VAT at 15%	15.00
Total due	115.00

Date (tax point)	Invoice number	Customer (name)	Gross amount	VAT	Net Standard Rate Goods/Services	Zero Rated Goods/Services	Exempt or Out of Scope Goods/Services
			£	£	£	£	£
					...		

Figure 9. *Sales Invoice Register*

The distinction of zero rate is important only because a trader who sells zero rated goods can still recover VAT charged to him, on, say, petrol expenses for business purposes even though he has no VAT to pay over to the Customs & Excise on his zero rate sales. He would not be able to do this if he were selling one of the few items which are exempt or outside the scope of VAT.

You can find out the goods and services which come under each category by asking your local VAT Office to give you a copy of VAT Notice 'Scope and Coverage'.

Retail schemes

In order to solve the problem outlined above, the retail schemes have been devised to allow you to calculate the correct amount of output tax in each VAT quarter.

There are nine schemes available and to some degree the individual trader has the choice of which to use. They are described later in this chapter.

The trader's choice is, however, restricted by certain over-riding criteria which are detailed below:

1. If all your sales are standard rated you must use Scheme A.
2. To use Scheme F you must be able to identify whether each individual item sold is standard rated or zero rated, usually by the use of separate totals on an electric till.
3. If your annual turnover (Sales) is more than £75,000 you cannot use Scheme C. Also, your Trade Classification number must lie between 8201 and 8239. This code number describes the type of trade that you are engaged in as determined by the Customs & Excise. You must also account separately for the VAT on any services that you supply if you use this scheme.
4. If your annual turnover is more than £200,000 you cannot use Scheme D. Again, any services that you supply must be accounted for separately if you use this scheme.
5. If you use Scheme B, the following must apply:

   (a) There must be no more than two rates of tax. Zero counts as a rate of tax and, therefore, if there is one standard rate and a zero rate, as currently operated in this country, then Scheme B could be used, provided that the following criteria are met.

      (i) Takings/Sales to which the lower rate of tax applies must be no more than 50 per cent of your total sales.

(ii) Any services that you supply at the higher of the two tax rates may be included in the scheme calculation, but any at the lower rate of tax must be accounted for separately.

6. If your annul turnover is less than £200,000 you cannot use Scheme G.

ustoms & Excise may also not allow you to use the scheme that you oose and may order you to use another, but this rarely happens.

Most small businesses involved in the retail schemes will probably find at the most convenient scheme to choose will be either Scheme A if all les are standard rated, or Scheme D.

I shall therefore deal with these two Schemes in detail and show the orkings for the others as an Appendix to this chapter, see page 76.

etail scheme A

is is the simplest scheme of all but can only be used where all sales are the standard rate of VAT.

To calculate the total output tax which is deemed to be included in ur total Takings you apply the following formula to the total Takings/ les for the period concerned.

$$\text{utput tax} = \text{Takings/Sales Total} \times \frac{\text{Standard VAT Rate}}{100 + \text{Standard VAT Rate}}$$

ppose that your VAT quarter ends on 31 March. How much output x is due for the period 1 January to 31 March (three months)? If the takings each month are as follows:

		£
nuary	=	5,000.00
bruary	=	6,000.00
arch	=	6,500.00
		£17,500.00

en the output tax due (assuming a standard rate of 15 per cent) is:

$$2,282.61 = £17,500.00 \times \frac{15}{100 + 15} \text{ or } \frac{3}{23}$$

herefore, £2,282.61 is the figure that would appear in Box 1 of the VAT eturn as shown on page 72.

Retail scheme D

If your sales records do not show which individual items are standard rated and which are zero rated and your turnover is less than £200,00 per annum, you can arrive at the output tax figure for each VAT quarter by using a calculation based on the proportion of standard rated good bought for resale to the total goods bought for resale. This is known a Scheme D.

The trick here is to prepare records of your purchases which separat out the various components that are required. Figure 10 (on page 7) shows how to set out a Purchase Invoice Register into which you shoul enter in date order the purchase invoices that you receive from you suppliers.

At the end of each VAT quarter you then add up the separat columns and prepare the following calculation using the resul obtained:

$$\text{Output tax} = \frac{\substack{\text{Standard Rate goods} \\ \text{for resale (inc VAT)}}}{\substack{\text{Total goods for} \\ \text{resale (inc VAT)}}} \times \text{Turnover} \times \frac{\substack{\text{Standard} \\ \text{VAT Rate}}}{\substack{100 + \text{Standard} \\ \text{VAT Rate}}}$$

As an example, suppose that your Total Sales amounted to £3,000 an that your Purchases are as set out in Figure 10. The output tax du would be calculated as follows:

$$\text{Output tax} = \frac{\text{Col 3} + \text{Col 8}}{\text{Col 3} + \text{Col 8} + \text{Col 4}} \times 3,000.00 \times \frac{15}{115}$$

$$£117.66 = \frac{187 + 28}{187 + 28 + 500} \times 3,000.00 \times \frac{15}{115}$$

Therefore, the figure that would appear in Box 1 of the VAT Retur would be £117.66.

In practice the totals of the Purchase Register for the three month ending on the date of the VAT Return are put into the above formul and applied to the sales for those three months.

Completing your VAT return

The VAT Return is a form which Customs & Excise send out to all VA registered traders at three monthly intervals. The basic layout of th form is shown in Figure 11 (on page 72).

Figure 10. *Purchase Invoice Register*

Date	Invoice number	Supplier (name)	Total amount £	VAT on Goods/Expenses £	Net Standard Goods for Resale £	Zero Rated Goods for Resale £	Net Standard Expenses £	Zero Rated Expenses £	Exempt items £	VAT on Goods for Resale £
2/3	1	Fred	100	13	87					13
5/3	2	Joe	115	15	100					15
10/3	3	Rates	1,000						1,000	
12/3	4	George	500			500				
15/3	5	Petrol	115	15			100			
20/3	6	Broker	200					200		
			2,030	43	187	500	100	200	1,000	28
Column			1	2	3	4	5	6	7	8

Figure 11. *Return of Value Added Tax*

Return of Value Added Tax

For the period   Vat Registration No

.... to ....

Name & Address of Registered Person

....

VAT due on Outputs   1 [   ]

Under-declarations of VAT not notified
in writing by Customs & Excise   2 [   ]

Total Output Tax Due   3 [(1 + 2)   ]

VAT deductible on Inputs   4 [   ]

Over-declarations not notified in
writing by Customs & Excise   5 [   ]

Total Input Tax Deductible   6 [(4 + 5)   ]

NET VAT PAYABLE OR REPAYABLE   7 [(3 − 6)   ]

Pay by Credit Transfer [ ] [ ]   Net Outputs 8 [   ]

Payment enclosed – – – –⁄

Repayment Due – – – –[ ]   Net Inputs 9 [   ]

Box 5 includes Bad Debt Relief (a)
Box 8 includes Exempt Outputs (b)   [(a)] [(b)] [(c)]
Box 8 includes Exports   (c)

Retail Scheme | A | B | C | D | E | F | G | H | J |

I: (Full Name in Block Letters)   declare that the information given in this
Return is true and complete.

Signature: ....   Date: ....

HOW TO PREPARE VAT RECORDS AND COMPLETE A VAT RETURN

The object of the exercise is to arrive at the amount of VAT that you re required to pay over to Customs & Excise which is simply the total tput tax less the total input tax for the quarter.

We have already seen on page 59 onwards how to go about obtaining e correct output tax figure which goes in Box 1.

Input tax, which goes in Box 4, is obtained from your purchase and penses invoices where you have obtained goods and services from AT registered suppliers.

If you pay for these goods and services immediately upon receipt then u can simply obtain the input tax figure direct from the VAT column your Cash Book as explained on page 61.

If you take credit for the goods that you buy, however, then you will ed to keep a Purchase Invoice Register along the lines described in igure 10 so that you are able to claim credit for the VAT suffered as on as you receive the goods and invoice, instead of waiting until you ay for them.

It must be emphasised that you can only claim input tax on invoices hich display a VAT registration number.

Some invoices, particularly petrol receipts, show only the total nount payable. The VAT is not shown separately. To find the amount VAT included you multiply the total figure by the standard rate of AT and divide the result by 100 plus the standard rate of VAT.

xample
n a total of £115 the VAT is:

$$15 \times \frac{15}{(100 + 15)} = 15$$

f the standard rate of VAT is 15%)

for any reason you discover an error in a previously prepared VAT eturn and the amount concerned is small in relation to your normal uarterly VAT bill, you can correct the error by entering the amount nder- or over-stated in Boxes 2 or 5 as appropriate. This amount will be dded to the output tax if the error is an amount of understated tax, or dded to the input tax if the opposite has occurred.

Any large errors should be reported direct to your local VAT Office writing.

Having completed Boxes 1 and 4 (and 2 and 5 if necessary), you then dd Box 1 to Box 2 and put the result in Box 3. Add Box 4 to Box 5 and ut the result in Box 6.

The VAT due to be paid over is the difference between Box 3 and Box 6 which is entered in Box 7.

If your input tax claim is greater than the total of Box 3 then Customs & Excise will refund money to you. In this case the figure in Box represents the amount that you are due to receive. Such an amount would be paid direct to your bank account.

There are two remaining boxes on the Return: 8 and 9.

Box 8 is for you to enter the net value, after deducting input tax, of your Sales for the quarter. You should also enter any VAT-exempt business income, such as rents received. If you have given cash discounts you should add them back to the Sales figure for the purposes of completing Box 8.

Box 9 shows the net of VAT value of all business purchases and expenses but leaving out the following:

(a) Wages/Salaries
(b) PAYE and National Insurance
(c) Drawings and Cash introduced
(d) Loans, dividends, grant, gifts of money
(e) Compensation payments or insurance claims
(f) Stock Exchange dealings.

You can complete Boxes 8 and 9 leaving out any exempt transactions. This is known as Method A whereas the above method of calculation is known as Method B.

If you use Method A, then you must leave out of the boxes the following additional items:

- *Box 8*
  (a) Sales of cars on which you paid no VAT
  (b) Exempt outputs (Sales)

- *Box 9*
  (a) Exempt purchases
  (b) MOT fees and Vehicle Road Tax
  (c) Local authority rates
  (d) Purchases on which you cannot reclaim input tax.

If you use Method B and your Sales or Purchases amount to more than £50,000 per quarter on average (or £20,000 per month), then you must inform Customs & Excise by letter. If you change the basis of filling in Boxes 8 and 9 then you must also inform Customs & Excise by letter.

Having completed all the figures it remains to tick the appropriate box to indicate whether you are paying out VAT or whether you are due for a refund; tick the box showing that you wish to pay by credit transfer if this is the case; tick one or more of the three boxes shown if any of the following are applicable:

(a) Box 5 includes bad debt relief (see below)
(b) Box 8 includes exempt outputs
(c) Box 8 includes exports.

If you are a retailer and are using one of the retail schemes for calculating output tax then tick the lettered box applicable.

Finally, sign the declaration at the foot of the form, completing your name and dating the form, and send it to Customs & Excise in the envelope provided, together with your cheque (if you are paying VAT over) for the amount shown in Box 7.

Bad debt relief

If you have not received payment for goods and services on which you have previously paid output tax, it may be possible for you to recover the VAT paid over from Customs & Excise.

However, to do this, the debtor must be formally insolvent and not merely reluctant to pay you.

You should contact your local VAT Office if you believe that bad debt relief may be available to you.

Appendix

1. Record of Purchase Invoices required for operating Scheme B

Date	Invoice number	Supplier (name)	Total cost exc VAT	VAT	Total cost inc VAT	Profit to be made on goods	Estimated sales at the lower tax rate
			£	£	£	£	£
2/3	1	Fred	100	–	100	20	120
5/3	2	Jack	150	–	150	30	<u>180</u>
							300

Less: Stock Lost at Selling Price	–
Bad Debts	–
Other Reductions in Estimated Profit	<u>–</u>
Total Estimated Sales Value of Goods at the Lower Rate	<u>£300</u>

Calculation of output tax

Assume total gross takings are £500

	£
Total Gross Takings	500
Less: Lower Rate Sales Estimated (Zero Rate)	<u>300</u>
Estimated Sales at the Standard Rate	<u>200</u>

$$\text{Output Tax} = £200 \times \frac{\text{VAT Rate Standard}}{100 + \text{VAT Rate Standard}}$$

$$= £200 \times \frac{15}{115} = £26.08$$

NB. You will also require a Purchase Register of all purchase invoices, standard rate and zero rate in order to obtain your input tax figures.

. Purchase records required to operate Scheme C

Purchase Invoice Register:

Date	Invoice number	Supplier (name)	Cost of Standard rate goods for resale	VAT on Standard rate goods for resale	Cost of Zero rate goods for resale
			£	£	£
3/3	1	David	100	15	
4/3	2	Jack			130
7/3	3	Peter	200	30	—
			300	45	130
Add VAT			45		
			345		

Add mark-up as prescribed
or the goods by Customs
& Excise   40

Assumed Retail Value   £385

$$\text{Output Tax} = £385 \times \frac{\text{Standard VAT Rate}}{100 + \text{Standard VAT Rate}}$$

$$= £385 \times \qquad \frac{15}{115} \qquad = £50.22$$

Assuming that the standard rate of VAT is 15 per cent.

Again you would also need to keep a Purchase Invoice Register of all
purchase/expense invoices in order to arrive at the input tax figures.

3. Scheme E

You prepare a Purchase Invoice Register similar to Scheme B on page 76, but the record will show the Selling Price of Goods for Resale at each positive rate of tax (eg, higher than zero), including the VAT, instead of the selling price of goods only at the lowest rate of VAT.

Thus Scheme E can cope with more than one positive rate of VAT.

The output tax is obtained by multiplying the totals of the selling prices for goods at each rate of tax in the VAT period, by the appropriate VAT fraction.

So if the total selling price including VAT at the standard rate (currently 15 per cent) of goods bought in the period is £10,000, the output tax is:

$$£10,000 \times \frac{15}{115} = £1,304.35$$

4. Scheme F

The output tax figure is arrived at by multiplying the total standard rated takings per the till rolls by the standard rate of VAT and dividing by 100 plus the standard rate of VAT:

Example

$$\text{Output tax} = \frac{\text{Standard Rate}}{100 + \text{Standard Rate}} \times \frac{\text{Total Standard Rated}}{\text{Goods Sold}}$$

$$£15 = \frac{15}{100 + 15} \times £115$$

This scheme can be applied where there is more than one positive rate of VAT, but you must be able to identify which rate of tax applies to each individual item sold. This can be done by the more advanced electronic tills now available.

5. Scheme G

Prepare an Invoice Register for your purchases as shown in Figure 12 on page 79.

Figure 12. *Purchase Invoice Register for Scheme G*

Date	Invoice number	Supplier (name)	Total amount inc VAT	VAT on Goods and Expenses	Standard Rate Goods for inc VAT	3 quarters accum totals of col 3	Standard + Zero Goods for resale inc VAT	3 quarters accum totals col 5	Standard Rate Expenses excl VAT	Exempt Expenses
			1	2	3	4	5	6	7	8
Totals end of VAT quarter 1					A	A	Z	Z		
Totals end of VAT quarter 2					B	A+B	Y	Z+Y		
Totals end of VAT quarter 3					C	A+B+C	X	Z+Y+X		
Totals end of VAT quarter 4					D	B+C+D	W	Y+X+W		
Totals end of VAT quarter 5					E	C+D+E	V	X+W+V		

To work out the output tax figure follow this procedure:

(a) Total Gross Takings for this VAT quarter $\times$ $\dfrac{\text{Total of col 3 this period only} + \text{Total of col 4 to end of last period}}{\text{Total of col 5 this period only} + \text{Total of col 6 to end of last period}}$

(b) Multiply the result of (a) by $\dfrac{\text{Standard VAT Rate}}{100 + \text{Standard VAT Rate}}$

If Standard VAT Rate is 15 per cent the fraction is $\dfrac{15}{100 + 15}$

which is the same as multiplying by 3 and dividing by 23.

(c) Multiply the result of (b) by 9 and divide that result by 8.

(c) is your output tax figure for Box 1 of your VAT Return.

Finally, deduct from the total of columns 4 and 6 the totals of columns 3 and 5 respectively which arose three VAT quarters ago and then add to columns 4 and 6 the totals of the current VAT quarter of columns 3 and 5 respectively.

In this way the totals of columns 4 and 6 should always be the accumulated totals of the most recent VAT quarters.

If you have just started to use this scheme then you will not have three quarters' totals in columns 4 and 6 to use in the above calculations. Therefore, for the first three VAT Returns only, you add to columns 4 and 6 the cost to you, including VAT, of the goods for resale that you had in stock when you started using this scheme. On the fourth VAT quarter you ignore the Stock figure and prepare the calculation as described above.

NB. You may only use this scheme if your annual turnover exceeds £200,000. Also, you may not use this scheme for services that you provide, or for goods that you sell which you have grown, or made yourself.

6. Scheme H

This scheme is the same in terms of calculation as Scheme G which has been explained in detail, except that instead of columns, 3, 4, 5 and 6 showing Goods for Resale at cost to you plus VAT, in Scheme H those

lumns should show the expected retail prices, including VAT, of
oods for Resale.

Since the Gross Profit is therefore automatically taken up in this
heme it is not necessary to multiply the result at (c) in the Scheme G
lculation by 9 and divide it by 8.

When you have reached point (b), that is the output tax figure
quired in Box 1 of your VAT Return.

With this scheme you can account for goods which you have made or
own yourself, unlike Scheme G; but again, you cannot use this scheme
account for services that you provide.

Scheme J

his scheme is again based on expected selling prices of Goods for Resale
order to arrive at the output tax figure.

The calculation is similar to Scheme G but result (a) is achieved as
llows:

(a) Total Gross Takings for the VAT quarter $\times$ $\dfrac{\text{Expected selling prices of goods for resale since the beginning of the first VAT period inc VAT at Standard rate plus your standard rate stock (at ESP) at the start of the first VAT quarter}}{\text{Expected selling prices of goods for resale since the beginning of the first VAT period inc VAT on all goods for resale both Standard rated and Zero rated, plus total stock (at ESP) at the start of the first VAT quarter}}$

ESP = Estimated Selling Price
The rest of the calculation is as for Scheme H.

t the end of the fourth VAT quarter, you ignore the accumulated
xpected selling price totals used in the above calculation and start again
king the fifth quarter as the first quarter in the new year and
roceeding as before.

At the end of each four VAT quarters it is necessary to do an end-of-
ear adjustment to account for any over- or under-payments of output
x during the year.

Again, you cannot use Scheme J for services that you supply.

If you want to know more about this scheme or any of the other schemes for retailers outlined in this chapter, ask at your local VAT Office where details of the various schemes are freely available upon request.

Chapter 9

A Few Tips on Starting a Small Business

Many people appear to think that starting up a small business for themselves is difficult. In fact, to start up a small business which does not involve forming a limited company, is really quite straightforward.

The usual problem is to be able to keep that business going once it has been set up. In other words, before you fly into it and start spending money, make reasonably sure that you can earn a living out of whatever you choose to do. Detailed advice is contained in *Working for Yourself: The Daily Telegraph Guide to Self-Employment* and *Starting a Successful Small Business*, both published by Kogan Page.

If you are buying an existing business, make sure that you see at least the last three years' accounts to ensure that the current business is making money. It is usually advisable to ask your accountant to examine the accounts for you and report his findings. *How to Buy a Business*, published by Kogan Page, summarises the points to watch out for.

Make sure that you have already, or can raise, enough money to keep you going while you are trying to establish yourself. Many businesses fail in their first year through failing to ensure that enough initial capital is going to be available to cover the period when trade is being built up and cash flow is poor. More businesses founder through lack of ready cash than from lack of trade.

If possible, start your business in a small way, even from home, and build up steadily. In this way you can avoid additional overheads, such as rent of premises, which are going to drain away your funds before you can really get going. Do check beforehand that the lease on your home allows you to run a business from the address.

If you have been unemployed for over eight weeks, you may be able to obtain financial assistance from the government. You can find out the details of the Enterprise Allowance Scheme from the Department of Employment, the Small Firms Service, or the Citizens' Advice Bureau.

Find a good accountant. His advice will be well worth the expense.

Action to be taken on starting a small business

1. Inform the Inland Revenue in your area that you intend to start trading. You should complete a form called 41G which can be

obtained from any Tax Office or from your accountant. This gives certain simple information to the Inland Revenue so that they can find your previous tax records and give you a reference number which will be used to cover the tax affairs of your business.

2. If you have left employment to start in business and have paid some tax in the current year under PAYE, send your Form P.45 (the form that your employer gives you when you leave work) with the Form 41G to the Inland Revenue. You may be entitled to a refund of tax paid.

3. Write to the Department of Social Security to let them know that you are trading. If you earn more than a certain amount from your business each year, you will be liable to pay Class 2 National Insurance contributions. The DSS will advise you what you need to do and how to make payments if you are liable to pay. If your annual profits exceed a certain sum, you will also be liable to pay Class 4 contributions.

4. Telephone or write to your local Customs & Excise VAT Office and ask them to tell you what the VAT limitation limits are for the year in which you start trading. If you are likely to exceed the turnover limits for the year then you will need to register for VAT. Customs & Excise will send you the appropriate forms on request.

5. If you need to employ someone in your business, write to or telephone the local Inland Revenue Office and they will advise you what you need to do.

If you go to an accountant from the outset, he should advise you on all the above points and will be able to supply all the necessary forms.

A warning about taxation of businesses

A lot of people think that because no tax is actually paid in the first 12 months of trading, there is no liability to pay tax on the profit earned in that period.

This is not the case. You would normally trade for 12 months and then have your accounts prepared by your accountant who would submit those accounts to the Inland Revenue.

The Inland Revenue then send you a bill for the amount of tax that is due on the agreed profits. The assessment is worked out under what is known as Schedule D and the essence of the Schedule is that tax is normally paid on the profit that you earned in the previous year. This enables the Inland Revenue to send you half of your tax bill for payment on 1 January each year and the second half is due for payment on 1 July of the same year. In the opening year, of course, there is no previous year, the profits assessed are those for the first 12 months' trading. The second year's tax is also based on the first 12 months' trading and similarly for the third year, after which time the previous year basis would normally start to operate.

In view of this peculiar way of doing things, it is a good idea, if possible, to show as small a profit as possible in the first 12 months because you will be taxed on that profit for at least the next two years.

I must point out that Schedule D taxation in all its intricacies is a very complicated subject, particularly if you make a loss. You would be very well advised to leave your tax affairs in the hands of a competent accountant.

One other point that sometimes takes people by surprise is that if you earn profits above a certain level, the Inland Revenue will send you a bill for Class 4 National Insurance on top of the income tax bill. This amount is in addition to normal weekly or monthly Class 2 National Insurance.

Ask your accountant to estimate how much tax you are likely to have to pay over a 12-month period and try to put aside regular amounts in order to cover that potential bill. That way you will not be out of pocket completely when the bill comes through the door, as so many people are.

Chapter 10

Further Reading from Kogan Page

Big Profits from Small Companies, Steven D Popell

Buying a Shop, The Daily Telegraph Guide, A St John Price

Financial Management for the Small Business, The Daily Telegraph Guide, Colin Barrow

The Guardian Guide to Running a Small Business, 7th edn, Clive Woodcock

How to Buy a Business, The Daily Telegraph Guide, Peter Farrell

How to Choose Business Premises: A Guide for the Small Firm, Howard Green, Brian Chalkley and Paul Foley

Law for the Small Business, The Daily Telegraph Guide, 6th edn, Patricia Clayton

Raising Finance, The Guardian Guide for the Small Business, 3rd edn, Clive Woodcock

The Small Business Action Kit, John Rosthorn, Andrew Haldane, Edward Blackwell and John Wholey

Sources of Free Business Information, Michael J Brooks

Starting a Successful Small Business, M J Morris

Understand Your Accounts, 2nd edn, A St John Price

Working for Yourself, The Daily Telegraph Guide to Self-Employment, 10th edn, Godfrey Golzen

Index

INDEX